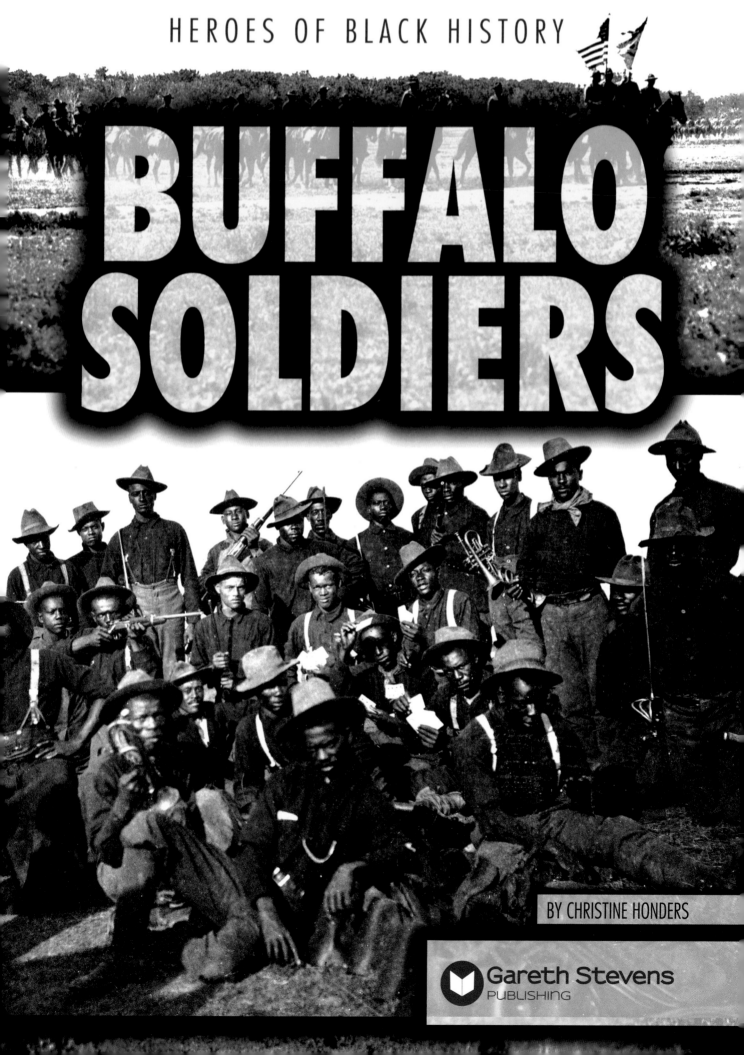

BUFFALO SOLDIERS

BY CHRISTINE HONDERS

Gareth Stevens
PUBLISHING

Please visit our website, www.garethstevens.com. For a free color catalog of all our high-quality books, call toll free 1-800-542-2595 or fax 1-877-542-2596.

Library of Congress Cataloging-in-Publication Data

Honders, Christine.
 Buffalo soldiers / Christine Honders.
    pages cm. — (Heroes of black history)
 Includes index.
 ISBN 978-1-4824-2900-8 (pbk.)
 ISBN 978-1-4824-2901-5 (6 pack)
 ISBN 978-1-4824-2902-2 (library binding)
 1. United States. Army—African American troops—History—Juvenile literature. 2. African American soldiers—History—Juvenile literature. 3. United States—History, Military—Juvenile literature. I. Title.
 E185.63.H66 2015
 973.8—dc23

                                    2014047869

First Edition

Published in 2016 by
Gareth Stevens Publishing
111 East 14th Street, Suite 349
New York, NY 10003

Copyright © 2016 Gareth Stevens Publishing

Designer: Katelyn E. Reynolds
Editor: Therese Shea

Photo credits: Cover, p. 1 US Army/National Archives/The LIFE Picture Collection/Getty Images; cover, pp. 1–32 (background image), 28 Signaleer/Wikipedia.com; pp. 5, 11 MPI/Getty Images; p. 7 Chr. Barthelmess/Library of Congress/Wikipedia.com; p. 9 (poster) Kean Collection/Getty Images; p. 9 (Edward Hatch) Civil War Photograph Collection/Library of Congress/Wikipedia.com; p. 13 Mai/Mai/The LIFE Images Collection/Getty Images; p. 15 Hulton Archive/Getty Images; p. 16 Bain News Service/Library of Congress/Wikipedia.com; p. 17 National Archives/The LIFE Images Collection/Getty Images; p. 19 (top) U.S. Army Military History Institute/NPS; p. 19 (bottom) T. Preiser, Special Collection, Suzzallo Library, University of Washington/NPS; p. 21 Library of Congress; p. 23 Afro American Newspapers/Gado/Getty Images; pp. 25 (top), 27 Time Life Pictures/National Archives/The LIFE Picture Collection/Getty Images; p. 25 (both bottom) Lucien Edmond/Wikipedia.com.

Printed in the United States of America

CPSIA compliance information: Batch #CS15GS: For further information contact Gareth Stevens, New York, New York at 1-800-542-2595.

CONTENTS

Words in the glossary appear in **bold** type the first time they are used in the text.

BUFFALO SOLDIERS

There's a long history of African Americans serving in the US military. They've fought in US wars since the conflict that established the country, the American Revolution (1775–1783). Most black people didn't have their personal freedom, but this didn't stop them from fighting for freedom from the British.

The first official black **regiments** had the nickname "buffalo soldiers." In nearly 85 years of service, buffalo soldiers participated in almost 200 events on the western **frontier**. They were also sent to Cuba, the Philippines, and Mexico. These men showed great courage by facing dangers in military service as well as facing great **prejudice** in their own country.

THE FIRST INTEGRATED US MILITARY?

The Continental army, which fought for the new nation against the British during the American Revolution, had so many black and white troops that a French soldier described them as "speckled." Sadly, American military forces wouldn't be nearly as **integrated** again for another 170 years.

This picture shows buffalo soldiers riding on horseback in the 1880s.

5

BLACK SOLDIERS IN THE CIVIL WAR

During the American Civil War (1861–1865), African Americans weren't allowed to join the regular US army. However, nearly 180,000 black men fought in **volunteer** regiments. Many of the black army units had outstanding combat records.

In July 1866, Congress organized six **segregated** regiments in the US Army, which later became four all-black regiments: the 9th and 10th **Cavalries** and the 24th and 25th **Infantries**.

NO WOMEN ALLOWED

Cathay Williams was the first black female soldier. Women weren't allowed to fight in the army, so she used the name "William Cathay" and never revealed she was female. She joined the army in 1866, claiming she was a 22-year-old cook, and served for 2 years.

There are several stories about how these soldiers became known as buffalo soldiers. One reports Native Americans thought the soldiers' hair looked like buffalo hair. Another says Native Americans gave them this name out of respect, because they were fierce and fought like buffalo.

Some soldiers in the 25th Infantry are shown here in coats made of buffalo hide. This may be another reason they were called buffalo soldiers.

PREJUDICE IN THE ARMY

Even though African Americans could now join the army, Congress decided their officers had to be white. There was a lot of prejudice against the black community, and some white officers refused to command black soldiers. Colonel Edward Hatch and Colonel Benjamin Grierson were the first to lead the 9th and 10th Cavalries.

At first, the buffalo soldiers were sent to posts in the western states. The army often gave them failing equipment and less **ammunition** than they needed. They had older, slower horses and poor quality food. However, the buffalo soldiers were more **disciplined** than other units. They also had the lowest desertion rate in the US Army.

UNCLE SAM WANTS YOU!

Joining the army sounded good to many African American men at that time. Black soldiers were paid $13 a month. This was much more than blacks could expect to make outside of the military. They were also given food, clothing, and a place to live, the same as white soldiers.

8

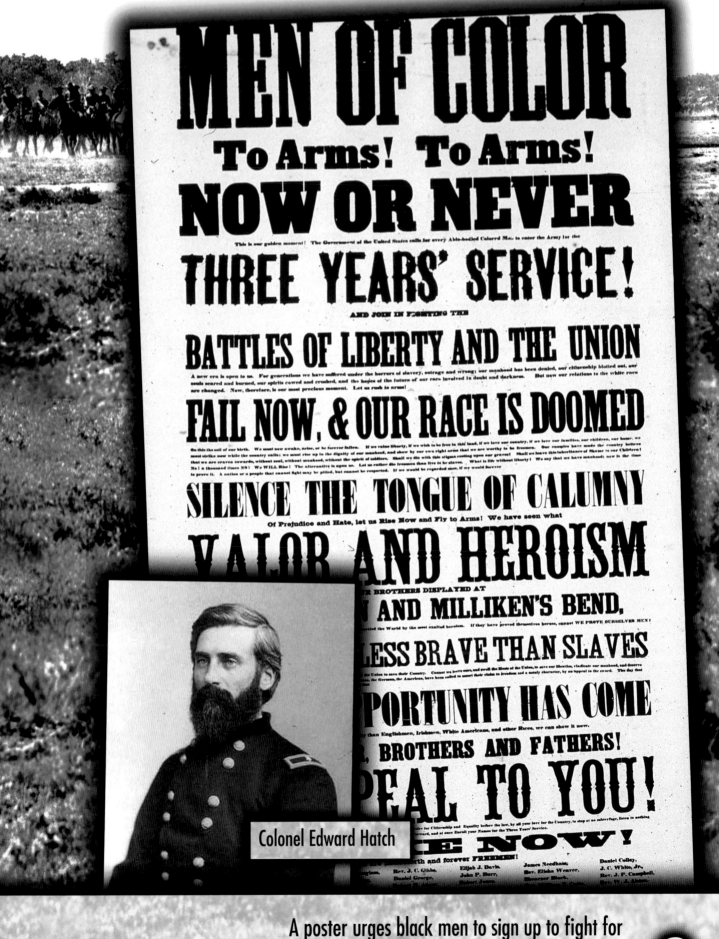

Colonel Edward Hatch

A poster urges black men to sign up to fight for the Union during the American Civil War. It warns that a Union defeat meant the black race was "doomed."

ON THE WESTERN FRONTIER

In 1867, the buffalo soldiers sent to western states had one main mission: to control the Native Americans of the Great Plains and Southwest. Many tribes were resisting being forced onto reservations, which were lands set aside for them. White settlers were taking over their historical lands. Buffalo soldiers fought in over 125 conflicts with Native American tribes, including the Cheyenne, Apache, and Sioux.

Buffalo soldiers were also responsible for the safety of stagecoaches, mail service, and trains through the West. They built forts, roads, and **telegraph** lines; mapped areas; and protected American settlers from outlaws and thieves.

A TOUGH JOB

Many buffalo soldiers were born into slavery. Some had relatives who had fled their slave masters and were welcomed into Seminole Indian tribes. This made it very hard for them to force Native Americans back to reservations. Buffalo soldiers understood what it was like not to have freedom.

This stagecoach is guarded by buffalo soldiers.

THE INDIAN WARS

The 9th and 10th Cavalries were stationed in Texas between the 1870s and 1890s during what were called the "Indian Wars." They fought in several battles against the fierce Apache, who were angry about being sent to live on reservations.

In one instance, buffalo soldier Sergeant Emanuel Stance noticed some Apache stealing horses from a government post near Kickapoo Springs, Texas. Stance and his patrol drove off the Apache after a long fight. Because of his bravery during this clash, Stance became the first professional black soldier to receive the Medal of Honor in June 1870.

SOLDIERS OF HONOR

Thirteen buffalo soldiers were awarded the Medal of Honor during the Indian Wars as well as six of their officers. Five buffalo soldiers received the Medal of Honor for their actions during the Spanish-American War (1898). Many others received the Certificate of Merit for acts of bravery above and beyond the call of duty.

12

The Medal of Honor was created during the American Civil War and is the highest honor given to a soldier.

HENRY O. FLIPPER

Henry Ossian Flipper was born into slavery in 1856. In 1873, he attended the US Military Academy in West Point, New York, and was the first black person to graduate from there. In 1878, Flipper became the first black officer in the US Army.

Flipper served in Company A of the 10th Cavalry in Texas and Oklahoma. At Fort Sill, Oklahoma, he oversaw the construction of a system that drained ponds surrounding the fort, which helped stop the spread of malaria, a deadly sickness at the time. This drainage system is called "Flipper's Ditch" and is now a national landmark.

WRONGLY ACCUSED?

Flipper dealt with prejudice during his career. In 1881, his commanding officer accused him of stealing money. He was found not guilty of stealing, but was **convicted** of "conduct unbecoming of an officer" and dismissed from the army. He died in 1940. In 1999, Henry Flipper was pardoned by President Bill Clinton.

Henry Ossian Flipper fought for the rest of his life to be reinstated into the army. He wrote a letter to Congress asking for "that justice which every American citizen has the right to ask."

THE BATTLE OF SAN JUAN HILL

The Spanish-American War began in April 1898. American troops, including more than 3,000 black soldiers, went to Cuba to fight for Cuba's independence from Spain. Many blacks in the United States wondered if buffalo soldiers should fight. Some US states were still segregated, and blacks who lived in these places didn't have equal rights.

Still, buffalo soldiers participated in the Battle of San Juan Hill on July 1, 1898. The 9th and 10th Cavalries and the 24th Infantry fought alongside white regiments, making it the most integrated battle of the nineteenth century. Twenty-six buffalo soldiers died. Several were honored for their bravery.

BLACK JACK

Lieutenant John J. Pershing (right) was a white officer in the 10th Cavalry at the Battle of San Juan Hill. He later wrote of the buffalo soldiers, "They fought their way into the hearts of the American people." Pershing was a strong supporter of black soldiers and was given the nickname "Black Jack" because of this.

The 9th Cavalry prepares to leave for Cuba in 1898.

THE PHILIPPINE-AMERICAN WAR

The Spanish-American War lasted just 10 weeks. The peace agreement included the United States taking control of the Philippines from Spain. Some Filipinos, called "insurectos," wanted independence from Americans, too. Buffalo soldiers were sent to the Philippines in 1899 to fight them.

Again, many in the black community thought it was unfair to send black troops to fight this war when they didn't have equal rights in the United States. Some insurectos even tried to convince black soldiers that they should abandon the United States. But many buffalo soldiers hoped that success in the Philippines would mean more respect at home.

LOYAL TO THEIR COUNTRY

The Filipinos gave flyers to the buffalo soldiers about how badly black people were treated in the United States and promised they would be rewarded if they joined the Filipinos. A few black soldiers joined them, but most remained loyal to the United States.

San Francisco 1900. En route to Philippines

These photos show Troop E (top) and Troop C (bottom) of the 9th Cavalry before they were sent to the Philippines.

CHARLES YOUNG

Charles Young was the third black person to graduate from the US Military Academy at West Point and to be made an army officer. He served on the western frontier, in the Spanish-American War, and in the Philippines. In 1903, Young became a company commander of the 9th Cavalry at the Presidio of San Francisco, California, a military post.

In May 1903, Captain Young and his soldiers received an exciting task. They were made the "guard of honor" for US President Theodore Roosevelt, leading him through the streets of San Francisco. This was the first time black soldiers were given this honor.

MAN OF MANY TALENTS

By the end of Young's career, he had become a colonel, the highest rank an African American had ever received. He was also a professor at Wilberforce University, an all-black college in Ohio, where he taught military science, French, and mathematics. Young directed the college band as well as played and wrote music for piano, violin, and guitar.

Charles Young, the first African American man to become a colonel, died on January 8, 1922, while in Nigeria.

21

PARK RANGERS

Six days after serving as President Roosevelt's guard of honor in San Francisco, Charles Young and his troops marched 323 miles (520 km) to Sequoia National Park. US soldiers had been managing California's parks during the summer since 1891, but black soldiers had never patrolled them before.

Young and the 9th Cavalry were responsible for protecting the forest and making sure people followed park rules. Soldiers took turns on forest fire watches. They also fixed park trails and built roads. In fact, in just one summer, the 9th built as much road as the soldiers did during the three previous summers combined!

PATROLLING THE PARKS

In the early 1900s, black people still faced prejudice every day. They were called names, beaten, even killed, and police officers often wouldn't help them. Many white people didn't like taking orders from African Americans, which made it hard for the soldiers to keep them from breaking laws.

22

Buffalo soldiers pose holding bugles and swords while at a camp in the early 1900s.

MEXICO AND WORLD WAR I

A civil war broke out in Mexico in 1910. In 1916, Mexican **revolutionary** Pancho Villa led a force into New Mexico, attacking and killing US citizens before fleeing back over the border. Brigadier General John J. Pershing led troops, including Charles Young and the 10th Cavalry, into Mexico to catch Villa. This was called the Mexican **Punitive** Expedition. The soldiers never caught Pancho Villa, but Mexican forces released 23 captured American troops.

When World War I started in 1914, buffalo soldiers weren't sent to Europe, again showing the prejudice against them. However, other black soldiers, including the 370th National Guard Infantry, were sent overseas to fight.

PRESIDENTIAL PREJUDICE

The 370th Infantry was made up of all black men, including its officers and commander, Colonel Franklin A. Dennison. However, President Woodrow Wilson didn't think that African Americans made good leaders, especially during wartime. Colonel Dennison was sent home from Europe and replaced with a white officer.

24

Buffalo soldiers in the 24th Infantry are shown below marching in the hunt for Pancho Villa.

Soldiers in the 370th National Guard Infantry are pictured above.

THE END OF MILITARY SEGREGATION

Many military commanders, like President Wilson, continued to think whites made better soldiers than blacks, even with the long record of bravery of the buffalo soldiers. In 1941, there were only five black officers in the whole army. African American soldiers in uniform even had to follow the unfair segregation laws in the South. During World War II (1939–1945), rather than allowing them to show their courage on the battlefield, the 9th and 10th Cavalries provided supplies to combat soldiers.

Finally, in 1948, the US Army made a big step towards integration. President Harry S. Truman declared that "there shall be equality of treatment and opportunity for all persons in the armed services without regard to race, color, religion, or national origin."

FIRST FOR EQUALITY

The US military gave its soldiers equal rights before the rest of the country was forced to. Between 1949 and 1951, black soldiers were integrated into white units for the first time. After 85 years, the story of the buffalo soldiers came to an end.

26

General John J. "Black Jack" Pershing inspects the 10th Cavalry in 1932.

27

HEROES OF THE MILITARY

General Colin Powell, the highest-ranking African American in military history, said the buffalo soldiers tested the "conscience of a nation." He meant that the United States asked them to fight and risk their lives for a country that wouldn't treat them equally. The bravery and honor of the buffalo soldiers forced the nation to see them as people who deserved the freedoms they were fighting to protect.

Today, blacks and whites serve together in all levels of the US military. The courageous role of the buffalo soldiers in helping to make this happen should never be forgotten.

HONORING THEIR LEGACY

More than 450 buffalo soldiers are buried in San Francisco National Cemetery. One is William Tompkins, who received the Medal of Honor during the Spanish-American War. He and other buffalo soldiers volunteered to dodge enemy fire in order to rescue American and Cuban soldiers.

A monument that honors the buffalo soldiers is located in Fort Leavenworth, Kansas.

TIMELINE OF THE BUFFALO SOLDIERS

1866 Congress creates six segregated army regiments of black soldiers in the US Army, which become four all-black regiments.

1867 The buffalo soldiers are sent to the western frontier.

1870 Sergeant Emanuel Stance becomes the first black soldier to receive the Medal of Honor.

1878 Henry O. Flipper becomes the first black officer in the US Army.

1898 Buffalo soldiers fight in the Battle of San Juan Hill in Cuba.

1899 Buffalo soldiers are sent to the Philippines to fight the insurectos.

1903 Captain Charles Young and other buffalo soldiers escort President Theodore Roosevelt through San Francisco. They later march to Sequoia National Park.

1916 General John J. Pershing leads buffalo soldiers in the Mexican Punitive Expedition.

1944 The 9th and 10th Cavalries provide supplies and services to soldiers during World War II.

1948 President Harry Truman passes a law that soldiers will receive equal rights.

1951 The last of the buffalo soldiers are integrated into other units.

GLOSSARY

ammunition: bullets, shells, and other things fired by weapons

cavalry: the part of the army made up of soldiers trained to fight on horseback

convict: to prove that someone is guilty of a crime in a court of law

disciplined: behaving in such a way that shows a willingness to obey rules or orders

frontier: a part of a country that has been newly opened for settlement

infantry: soldiers trained to fight on foot

integrated: open to all people

prejudice: an unfair feeling of dislike for a person or group because of race or other features

punitive: intended to punish someone or something

regiment: a military unit made up of smaller military units

revolutionary: describing someone who works to overthrow an established government

segregated: forcibly separated into races or classes

telegraph: a method of communicating using electric signals sent through wires

volunteer: offering service without being asked

FOR MORE INFORMATION

BOOKS

Garland, Sherry. *The Buffalo Soldier*. Gretna, LA: Pelican Publishing, 2006.

Glaser, Jason. *Buffalo Soldiers and the American West*. Mankato, MN: Capstone Press, 2006.

WEBSITES

Buffalo Soldiers
www.tshaonline.org/handbook/online/articles/qlb01
Read a brief history of the buffalo soldiers on this Texas history website.

The Buffalo Soldiers
www.nps.gov/prsf/historyculture/buffalo-soldiers.htm
Read a complete history with photos of the buffalo soldiers.

Buffalo Soldiers & Indian Wars
www.buffalosoldier.net
Find out more about the buffalo soldiers in the Indian Wars of the 1800s.

INDEX